Peering Through The Mist

A Collection of Poetry
By
Jeff Whitehead
&
Darren Whitehead

First Published June 2008
By
We Done It Publishing.

Copyright © Jeff Whitehead & Darren Whitehead.
All rights reserved.

Jeff & Darren Whitehead have asserted the moral right to be identified as joint authors of this work.

A catalogue right for this book is available from The British Library.

ISBN 978-0-9558576-0-7

Contents

Acknowledgements   4

Childhood:

Memories   7
Dawning   8

Thicker Than Water:

Belief   11
Dad   12
Mum   13
Chameleon ... She Blushes   14

Lost in the Wilderness:

They Came Too Late   17
Deer's Mourn   18
The Crying Hare   19
Concrete Prairie   20

Fear:

Death of a Nightmare   23
One Man's Fear   24
Slamming Doors   25 - 26

Toils:

Miracle of Deliverance   29
Unchained Melody   30
Not a Word   31
Flicking Back The Pages   32

Betrayal:

Priorities   35
Breath   36
The Way The Second Hand Ticks   37
Baggage   38 - 39

... And Then The Clock Stopped:

I hear the Lark   43
Echoes   44
Our Brother   45

Hobson's Final Choice:

Somewhere New   49
Kissing His Mind   50
Cold Night Air   51

Zen:

Sea of Zen   55
The Purpose   56
Suddenly   57

Just Like That!

Brenda   61
Adult Lessons   62 - 65
Old Grey Whistle   66
Slurping   67
Did I Just Say That?   68 - 69
Thank Heathens for Festivity   70 - 71
My daughter is an Angel   72
Flat Caps & Braces   73
Miss Me Madly   74
Rebel Without a Clue   75

Acknowledgement by Jeff Whitehead

Without the help and contributions from my son, Darren, I wouldn't have had the inspiration to go through with the publication of this book.

I also offer sincere thanks for the loving support of Darren's mum, my wife, Norma Whitehead who always encourages us to work as a team.

Acknowledgement by Darren Whitehead

Of course, this book would not be complete without due acknowledgement to my parents, Norma and Jeff who have supported me through thick and thin throughout the years. Even now, as a grown man, they are there for me and have always inspired me to be who I am. I would draw your attention to the poems on pages 12 & 13 of this book. I mean every word.

Childhood

Memories

When life was new and fresh
Will forever store
Memories that I cherish

Shadows lengthen, sink to rest.
Houses follow winding course,
Shaded white on hill's crest

Hush of mid-day forest
Sweet taste of orange grove
Memories that I cherish

Singing streams caress
Serene love sky
Shades of white on hill's crest

Memories alive and fresh,
In this tiny alcove
Memories that I cherish

Within the orange grove
When life was new and fresh
Memories that I cherish

Jeff Whitehead

Dawning

Enveloped by warmth,
Held lovingly by
Sheets crisp.

Existence is nothing
Sensual is all

Unaware of the heartbeat in my ears

Light beams disturb,
Yet tepidly stroke
Snug soma
Exposed.

Unbornly lying
Unaware of ticking clock.

Timeless time passes unnoticed
Until my time
Arrives.
Ten more cozy minutes
Won't take that away
In spite of my thoughtless hopes.

With newborn puppy eyes I arrive,
As if for the first time.

The sting
From womb to world
Encourages my retreat back
To crisp sheet.

Another dawning.
I tardily turn
To leave sheets crisp
Behind.

Darren Whitehead

Thicker Than Water

Belief

You didn't show your disappointments
Your tears
Your worries, your hidden torment
Your fears
Your struggles to make ends meet
Your fate
Your trials to keep him sweet
Your mate

You couldn't hide, the silent smile
Your caring love
Your song of praise, of father's style
The way he kept life fresh
And promised
You happiness

Jeff Whitehead

Dad

The strongest man I have ever known,
Strength of loyalty and pride.
A man, who fools he will not stand,
With honest bluntness loves those near.
Never one to stop and fail
And always true to self respect.

With fierce commitment, he'll protect
Those loves and things he calls his own.
With determination to prevail
Setbacks taken in his stride.
Not often one to shed a tear
But one to give a guiding hand.

A man who often will demand
Standards that are near perfect.
Not often one to show his fear
To only those the closest shown.
A man with burning fire inside.
Never allowed his time to stale

In his wake a charcoal trail
Of memories at his command.
Never one to step aside,
Or let a man show disrespect.
Through him many men have grown
And learned to gladly persevere.

Never one to disappear
From any challenge or small detail.
A sort of man who's always prone
To build his knowledge and expand.
His word is truth, his word direct.
Strong within and tough outside.

Always happy to provide
For those he loves and holds most dear.
Often one to self reflect
And ready to rewrite the tale.
Strong and able to withstand
Anything bad luck has blown.

A man I love, a man I hail.
One I respect and learn from and
One I call Dad, just him alone.

Darren Whitehead

Mum

The kindest eyes I have ever known,
Show me that I'm not alone.

One who cares, who always will
To thaw my soul in winter chill.

As gentle as a snowdrop kiss,
So many smiles to reminisce.

With warmest heart and kindest smile.
One who makes me feel worthwhile.

She reads me like an open book,
Knows my thoughts with just one look.

Quick to praise and quick to guide,
Always standing by my side.

Helps my struggles, shares my pain,
Shelters me from pouring rain.

Yet hides her pain so I don't see,
For she cannot bear to burden me.

She loves with no conditions set,
Hides her tears when she's upset.

Giving, selfless, like no other,
My dearest, darling, gorgeous mother.

An angel with a loving hand,
Who's always there to understand.

She's helped me be who I've become.
I'm proud to call this angel, Mum.

Darren Whitehead

Chameleon ... She Blushes

Silence awaits debate, none
No matter, love gone, just gone
Chameleon... she blushes

One-sided sorrow eats deeper
Involuntary tear
Irrelevant words; not what she wishes to hear
Chameleon... she blushes

He touches, acquiring information
She cringes, retracts
His responsive actions diminish, crack
Chameleon ... she blushes

He wants to ease her pain
Stroke away the tear
Defend her heart
Soothe away the fear
Chameleon... she blushes

The times her sweet tears
Had soaked and stained his shirt
The times he'd kissed her knee
Rubbed away the hurt
Chameleon... she blushes

The years wafted away
His baby girl she's grown
Deserted by a husband
A little girl of her own
Chameleon... she blushes

Still her daddy's girl

Jeff Whitehead

Lost in the Wilderness

They came too late.

He clasped his blooded neck with shocked round eyes.
Scarlet liquid decanted to the floor.
They came too late to hear his woeful cries.

He tried to flee but running was unwise.
His legs just couldn't hold him anymore.
He clasped his blooded neck with shocked round eyes.

His vision blurred with horrible surprise.
With shattered hope he looked towards the door.
They came too late to hear his woeful cries.

He prayed to God, but naught was in the skies.
The devil's hound was thirsty now for more.
He clasped his blooded neck with shocked round eyes.

The hound was licking, drooling for its prize,
It crunched and ripped and growled and snarled and tore.
They came too late to hear his woeful cries.

The growls drowned out the sound of his demise.
They found him bathed in red upon the floor.
He clasped his blooded neck with shocked round eyes.
They came too late to hear his woeful cries.

Darren Whitehead

Deer's Mourn

Bone, muscle, shattered, torn.
Suspended, vultures hover
Wolves, blood stained jaws, deer's mourn

Dangling three month fawn
Shifting medley, of fearful bother
Bone, muscle, shattered, torn

Lingering ungainly, shadows in scorn
Trembling, helpless, mother
Wolves, blood stained jaws, deer's mourn

Blood seeped sandstorm,
Snapping, snarling wolves, vulture's unwieldy cover
Bone, muscle, shattered, torn

The fawn to die, was born
Didn't have a brother
Wolves' bloodstained jaws, deer's mourn

Unkempt, sand covered coats
The plains wild rovers
Bone, muscle, shattered, torn
Wolves' bloodstained jaws, deer's mourn

Jeff Whitehead

The Crying Hare

We rose with the winter sun
My dad and I
Old scruff sighs a sigh
Put our anoraks on
Ferret and a gun
The skylark soars up high
Ice cold light blue sky
Tractor engine hum

Moorland biting air
Bobbing cotton wool
My dad he aims the gun
Wounded crying hare
My eyes dampen full
Clouding winter sun

Jeff Whitehead

Concrete Prairie

Cowardly intimidators
Nervously gathered
False laughing.
Testosterone fuelled rituals
Of boyish manhood
Uniformed.
Hunter, hunted, eyes hooded, scan
Untamed hyena,
Or young man?

Darren Whitehead

Fear

Death of a Nightmare

Darkened walls,
In brightest light.
A place that Summer cannot warm.

Excited shoves
Within the crowd.
Returning scrambles warn
In panic.

Wild imaginations
Of dead cobweb stairs
Of charcoal eyes,
Of loose boards
Creaking doors
Slamming.

Thoughts of black captivity
Captivate and scare
The scrambling crowd
Of childhood shoves.

Unaware of inside
Believing the unbelievable.
Big brother's tales,
Of ladies grey
Waiting.

Of rocking chairs
And whispers.
Of death on strike of twelve.
Of photographs of figures, white
In highest window pane.
Of souls who ventured in
To not again return.

Replaced by time
By concrete
By car park
Shopping Mall

They killed our dreams
When they killed our nightmare.
The day that haunted
Fell.

Darren Whitehead

One Man's Fear

A lonely walk
Down echoed street.
Past teenage group
Stares at his feet.

Husband chased
By thoughts and strife
The worry of a cheating wife.
Woodpecker thoughts throughout his day
As time away is time to play.

To release the hand
To pace the floor
When only child
Plays beyond the door.

Monster fears
Newpapers' friend.
Tabloid feeds the fear
Of men.

A soldier's mum
At News at Ten.
Holding breath
Each night again.

Target missed
A deadline gone
Invaded dreams,
Insomnolent bomb.

Stockbroker's heart
About to burst.
As Wall Street crashes
Dumps him headfirst.

Crumpled man
In lonely home
Confused and scared
To die alone.

One man's fear,
Another's fate.
Fear of fate
Instilled, innate.

Darren Whitehead.

Slamming Doors

Clunk, door slams behind me
Pipes grumble, hiss
Skittering paws in damp mist
Smell of rats and cats
Skitter, skitter screech
Smoky licks his lips

Smoky licks his lips
Green eyes glare at me
As rusting hinges screech
Lingering spits and hisses
Battered head of alley cat
Peering through the mist

A shadow drawls within the mist
Blooded fangs and lips
Victorious purring cat
Still watching me
Grumbling pipes hiss
Clawed flesh, rat's last screech

Invisible turning wheels screech
Ghostly noises within the mist
Voices whispering hush and hiss
Cold sweat and dry lips
Burned dead haunting me
Cross my path black alley cat

Snarling, growling, spitting cat
Ashes whirlwind, rafters screech
Burning embers follow me
Skeletons peer through the mist
Breathing shallow through silent lips

Dry throats, croaking hiss
Rusted steam pipes hiss
Kittens whine for mother cat
Smoky licks his lips

Skeletons begin to screech
Clamber through the mist
Watch-man's job just isn't me

With trembling lips I leave behind the screeching hiss
If you where me you'd do the same; I don't like cats
From cobbled street I still hear screech. I disappear in mist

Jeff Whitehead

Toils

Miracle of Deliverance

The brave English heroes plan our retreat.
Wincing as whistles graze by my head.
Will history judge these ten days as defeat?

Dressing in lines as we wait for the fleet.
A disciplined force but half of us dead.
The brave English heroes plan our retreat.

Polish and bull, shit we have to look neat?
"Give the men something to do", Major said.
Will history judge these ten days as defeat?

Standing like statues, the shattered elite.
Eyes shrapnel black and legs dead as lead.
The brave English heroes plan our retreat.

Backs to the channel we cannot compete.
The shells in the sea reiterate dread.
Will history judge these ten days as defeat?

Fire in the sky burns my face with the heat.
Empty men floating with love left unsaid.
The brave English heroes plan our retreat.
Will history judge these ten days as defeat?

Darren Whitehead

Unchained Melody

My time won't come. My time can't see
A better world, a world more kind.
The day my people will be free.

My days are shattered, stinging me.
Master's whip, I'm much maligned.
My time won't come. My time can't see

A place with love and harmony,
A world that's simply colour blind,
The day my people will be free.

No chafing chains, agreed decree,
No white man's boot or trader's mind.
My time won't come. My time can't see

The day I have my liberty,
A chequered earth, black white combined,
The day my people will be free.

Shackles are my destiny.
I'll die in irons, left behind.
My time won't come. My time can't see
The day my people will be free.

Darren Whitehead

Not a Word

Not a word, just tapping, hacking
Their names now, carved in stone
Or become ashes, away blown
Not a word just hacking tapping
Staring eyes, criminal looking faces, blacking
Men haunch, sinewy arms and muscles groan
Picks tap, panting breath, aching bone
Thick flying coal dust on lungs settling

Mysterious blackness heavy with gasses
Ghostly forms moved twisted, writhed
Gleaming whites of eyes, criminal looking faces
Dripping water, groans of fatigue
Only reddish points of light now seen
Not a word, just tapping, hacking.

Jeff Whitehead

Flicking Back The Pages

Building sheds, wooden blocks, rotting barge repaired.
Stagnant water gurgles over barges half submerged.
Weaving tentacles of weed drag them dark abode.
Nothing in this eerie place resembling modern mode.

Desolated unkempt paths, thistles, puddles, cracks.
Something haunting, weary snort, stops me in my tracks.
Clip-clop of metal shoes nothing to be seen,
Fragments of my bygone days, when I was just fourteen.

Steaming white lather, extractions of the strain.
Dragging forty tonnes a day, through wind and sleet and rain.
Distant disappearing sounds, a shiver to behold,
Picturing the bay mare resolute and so bold.

My mind flicks back the pages, of danger and dark cell.
Trapped beneath the real world, in pain, in fear, in hell.
Silvery yellow shining rays, bobbing patterned waves.
Left alone with skeletons in this foreboding grave.

Days go by, or are they nights? No sense of time at all,
Reality elusive, within that blackened wall.
A flash of light, a sense of hope, a young heart pounds and races.
Echoing sounds of picks and shovels the sight of blackened faces.

A hawk, it hovers then it swoops, distracting me from thought.
From it's beak drips the blood of a squirming mouse it caught.
Like the splintering pit props, swooping down from darkened sky.
Piercing dust stained flesh, blood spurting from my thigh.

Beyond it all wreckers await, a century's mutation.
14,000 tons of rubble, industrial revelation.
Shaft now level with the face, officials they've endorsed,
Candle lit caverns, and pit ponies have duly run their course.

A Temporary monument to the past, rusting wire ropes.
Redundant huge coal hopper stands within the coal dust slopes.
Twisted girders on a broken wall, balks of timber remain.
Ghostly figures and crippled men, the pits they were to blame.

As I cough the thick black and live on borrowed time,
From the soil seeps the blood of men killed in the mine.

Jeff Whitehead

Betrayal

Priorities 1

Car wreck,
Metal twisted,
Passenger, broken neck.
Unfinished text on blood stained 'phone.
Impact.

Priorities 2

Drunken
Empty bottle
Kids go hungry, dad drinks
Mummy's black eyes and daddy's lies
Gutter

Priorities 3

Swallow
Each gulp steals hope
Each lie, tear, hidden fear
Golden prospects ruined liver
Wasted

Priorities 4

Girlfriend
No time for friends
But sometimes girlfriends end
Forgotten friends are needed then
Humble

Darren Whitehead

Breath

Memories of soft hands and angel eyes.
Smiling at the thought of sweet breath
On nape of neck.

Golden band proudly worn
With contented smugness.

Early finish brings bouquet
In decorated hand
As silent key turns.

Creaking door drowned
By sweet breath
On nape of neck.

Muffled sounds, he hears
As married years
Are breathed away.

Floorboard alarm comes too late
As return comes too early
For sweet breath.

Sweet breath held,
As clutched blankets shield.

No one hears the discarded bouquet
As it drops in doorway
Winded.

Memories of soft hands and devil eyes.
Scowling at the thought of sweet breath
On another's neck.

Discarded trampled petals
Lie silently.
Resembling little of the flowers
They once were.

Only the sweet smell lingers
On bitter breath.

Darren Whitehead

The way the second hand ticks.

Memories of soft hands and devil eyes.
Scowling at the thought of sweet breath
On another's neck.

Betrayal spawned monster
With sharp tongue
And blunt fist.

Bitter green eyes,
Frightening windows to a soulless soul.

Pain turns to numbness
As sweet breath turns silent.

Numbness turns to pain
And bitter breath turns to gasp.

Heaving desperate rasps swallow air.
Green eyes study stained red fist.

Recent memories of screams echo
As if long gone.

The second hand turns only one way.

Unblinking blue eyes fix
On stained monster.

Betrayal spawns guilt.

Memories of fixed eyes haunt,
As the second hand turns
Stealing time.

Green eyes study clean, dirty hands
As second hand man sits
Pensive.

Ash box and ashes
Bare walls and bars
An unexpected destiny
The way the second hand ticks.

Darren Whitehead

Baggage:

The clock face stares back
As I wait.
The seconds drag, yet steal my precious time.
As I wait.
As I wait.

The life of an estranged father
Is tangled with guilt.

Competing affections of
A new love, a new life
A child not of my loins.

A smiling child hungry for affection,
Stomach rumbling in anticipation
Of a new love
A new life.

Will time ease the guilt I feel towards my own?
Will time make affection come more naturally?
For the seconds steal my precious time.
As I wait
As I wait.

But the clock never gives.
Just takes.
Just takes.

And now the time has come to bond with my own
And I await her arrival.
My stomach rumbling in knots of guilt
As I wait.
As I wait.

Her smiling face,
Her loose pony tails,
Her childish wit and exuberance
Wash the knot loose

And we laugh.
And we laugh.

Her giggles ignite in me a love that is not surrogate.

One so small yet strong enough to lift me higher than anyone can.
Strong enough to lift me.
To lift me.

Our time together precious
Stolen by the clock
As the seconds race away
Like falling water lost in the rapids
Water that I can never taste again.

And we play.
And we play.

Until the clock has stolen the time we had.
Until her giggles turn to goodbyes.

Like the rapids she rushes on,
Never looking back.

Takes for granted that goodbye kiss that she forces
When reminded.
Takes for granted the emptiness she leaves
In the silence of her wake.

And my stomach knots with guilt.

As I sigh.
As I sigh.

As I turn back,
To my new life.
To my new love.

As I turn back
But never turning my back on the giggles in the memory of my heart.

The life of an estranged father
Is tangled with guilt.

A carousel full of cases,
Travel worn
And bursting with guilt

Cases always dragged
Rarely lifted above knee height

Weighted with each lost second
With each stealthy tock
Each chime thickening my throat.

Thickening my throat.

Darren Whitehead

… And Then The Clock Stopped

I hear the lark

I hear the Lark in song
And stagger from my bed

This hazy spring morn
I watch life on wing

Fluttering like a sparrow
Weaving in breeze

Wood-smoke
Sweet smell of violet

Floats over cobbled
Farm-yard

From my birds eye view
My lady wipes away a tear

I fear she knows
My life soon, to disappear

My mirror of life
Now death

Jeff Whitehead

Echoes

Tick echoes after tock,
From the faithful clock.
The old timer
In the dusty room.

He watches ticks turn into years
Hears chimes echo
In deaf overgrown ears.

Threadbare clothes of yesteryears,
Bald at the elbows and knees.
Cobweb threads
Barely make ends meet.

Faded photos of children's children hide
Behind grease and nicotine.
Seeking their smiles with
Watery glass covered eyes.

Remembering forgotten memories
Of unforgotten faces.

Tracing with yellowed finger,
A brown faced reminder
Of a life that was
And one that is
Outside.

Gnarled knuckles weakly clutch,
Medals earned
That mean not much to outside.

Found in silent echoes of memories.
Through smoky uric air
Brown smiles witness
His last tock.

Tick echoes after tock,
From the dusty clock
In the silent room.

Darren Whitehead

Our Brother

Friday morning, we laughed
I didn't like that afternoon
Couldn't believe it happened so fast
Unexpected gloom

I didn't like that afternoon
All his good times slid past
Unexpected gloom
Fighting for his last

All his good times slid past
Dark clouds came at noon
Fighting for his last
Industrial dust and ruin

Dark clouds came at noon
Shadows of his death
Industrial dust and ruin
That afternoon our brother left

Shadows of his death
Too late to see it brewing
That afternoon our brother left
Industry filth took him

Too late to see it brewing
I didn't like that afternoon
Industry filth took him
Friday morning, we laughed

Jeff Whitehead

Hobson's Final Choice

Somewhere New

From each other's streaming eyes, they knew what they must do.
Peering through the tears, they found a sorry smile.
Would this be the last time that they whispered I love you?

Remembering their history and everyone they knew,
From when they found each other to walking down the aisle.
From each other's streaming eyes, they knew what they must do.

Fled torture and oppression to come to somewhere new.
To find their little angel a life that was worthwhile.
Would this be the last time that they whispered I love you?

They never fully settled and never quite knew who
To trust and share, to find as friends, or who would be hostile.
From each other's streaming eyes, they knew what they must do.

Their angel snatched and tortured, they'd hoped it was untrue.
Found cold and lifeless on a track, discarded by the vile.
Would this be the last time that they whispered I love you?

He said to her "I love you", she said she loved him too.
Time to join their angel. Found innocent at trial.
From each other's streaming eyes, they knew what they must do.
Would this be the last time that they whispered I love you?

Darren Whitehead

Kissing his Mind

Nothing more than bone and rags
Broken spectacles, he wore
Trod down shoes
Treasured photograph he owns
Lost dreams and broken mind
Glaring at dwindling flames, alone

In shadows he stooped alone
Thoughts, like tattered rags
His wife and daughter, kiss his mind
The kisses he still wore
He rambles, mumbles, on his own
Farewell to luck, symbolic horse shoe

The clipping heels of his wife's shoes
Screeching wheels, he cries alone
His wife's, his daughter's death, better if his own
Hopes, love, pride in rags
Haunting memories, sanity worn
Lost dreams, broken mind

Wrinkles of blonde, he sees in mind
Tiny feet in her mother's shoes
Pink dress and bow she wore
Disappear from misting eyes, leaving him alone
Nothing more than bones and rags
And the photograph he owns

Shivering wilderness his own
One thought left on mind
Like a tattered rag
Or like his worn out shoes
Red ashes twirl, he sits alone
A discarded thing out worn

Haunting memories, sanity worn
That haunting bloody night, faced on his own
The depth of one way thought, sat alone
Finality of death on his mind
Farewell the lucky horseshoe
From riches to the rag

Splashing, cold, alone, broken and worn
Gurgling rag, sinking bone, water claims as own
Drowning mind, sodden shoes

Jeff Whitehead

Cold Night Air

She hides and holds her son behind the chair.
"Be still, be calm, stay quiet, my little sweet"
She daren't go out and face the cold night air.

The shadowed figure knows that she is there.
He doesn't like the lies nor the deceit.
She hides and holds her son behind the chair.

He knows their fear, but simply doesn't care.
He raps the door and will not face defeat.
She daren't go out and face the cold night air.

The carcasses of mail are her despair.
She couldn't pay the bills, but had to eat.
She hides and holds her son behind the chair.

With streaky eyes, she holds her matted hair.
Reminders red will see her on the street.
She daren't go out and face the cold night air.

Through splintered door he comes to find a pair
Chilled bodies, pale and dead in their retreat.
She hides and holds her son behind the chair.
She daren't go out and face the cold night air.

Darren Whitehead

Zen

Sea of Zen

Between caravans and chalets,
I stroll tangled paths.
A warm sea breeze caresses.

Orange splashes from toppled can,
skew whiff wickets, cricket bats.
Cricket ball rolls under van.

Dusk is creeping near.
One by one they are summoned.
Despondent voices disappear.

Beneath red splashed sky,
flashes of light grey.
Seagulls dip, and cry.

From sea wall a cricket hums,
sand sweeps gently across my path.
I drift between dunes

My eyes half closed,
I drown in the Sea of Zen.
From silence, energy flows.

Jeff Whitehead

The Purpose

He is:
The tree with one branch
The first
The last drop of rain
Life before death
After death
Thought
Without thought

The breeze wove into him
He wove into the breeze
Like
An apparition
Weaving through the forest
Wispy beard
Drooping eyes
Staff
White ankle length robe
Swishes over rock
His feet slide over a bed of pebbles
Waves spew and splash
He kneels before the rock
The original faceless face

Jeff Whitehead

Suddenly

I reach out to grasp, the sound and smell
I feel no touch as I float through,
this arched array of colour
From this new planet where there is no limit
in time or space
I can see the sound of hymns.
I can hear the smell of each,
personal flower.
I can hear your tear fall
I touch your cheek.
Suddenly I hear your smile.
I answer yes.

Jeff Whitehead

Just Like That!

Brenda

Brenda, 60's chick
'Common as muck'
House a tip

Likes Blackpool, and works trip
Enjoys life too much
Brenda, 60's chick

Sticks fingers down throat, sick
Lager and lime, Babycham and such
House a tip

F's and blinds, lets it rip
Doesn't go to church much
Brenda, 60's chick

Leopard skin coat, hair bleached, slick
Has affairs, little slut
House a tip

Painted face, plenty lip
Bailiff's nightmare, keeps door shut
Brenda , 60's chick
House a tip

Jeff Whitehead

Adult Lessons:

I'm inside out,
I'm upside down
Find myself walking around.

I can't eat.
I can't eat.

I turn and toss
I can't even toss off
And they say that this is puppy love.

I can't sleep.
I can't sleep.

I'm early for class
When I used to be late
But when I'm there I just don't concentrate.

I can't think.
I can't think.

When I see you
I don't know what to say
I'll talk tomorrow, can't face today.

I can't speak.
I can't speak.

I watch you
Sitting across the room
I get a hard on when I smell your perfume

I daren't stand.
I daren't stand.

The other night
I dreamt of you
I wanna make love, but I don't know how to.

I won't tell.
Please don't tell.

I want to kiss you
I can hardly wait
But I'm scared that I'll ejaculate.

I can't touch.
I daren't touch.

I get your number
From a friend
I hear your voice and the phone call ends.

I hang up.
I'm hung up.

On Saturday
I walk past your street.
Twenty times aint too discreet.

I won't knock.
I can't knock.

I'll ask you Monday
Before assembly
That way the rest of the week is free

Of your thoughts.
Of your thoughts.

But Friday comes
The deeds not done
I can't face the whole weekend alone.

Just get it done.
Get it done.

I'll get my mate
To ask you out
That way I can get blown out

And I won't blush.
I might blush.

A resounding no
Echoes in my ears
I'll remember this f*****g day for years.

I might die.
I won't cry.

I see you on Saturday
With a lad who shaves
Got a motorbike and a pair of shades.

I can't compete
On the back seat.

He's like a man
I'm just a boy
He's a biker whilst I still play with toys.

It aint fair.
I've no body hair.

He has a beard,
While I have zits
He's got hair under his armpits.

I've got none,
Well ... Maybe one.

Now time's gone on
And I'm bald with bills
Found myself taking headache pills.

Just the one.
Just the one.

No hair on my head,
But growing out of my ears.
A few more wrinkles to go with the years.

One or two.
Just one or two.

No longer the pleasure
Of nightly wet dreams
Wake on the dot for a shift work regime.

Life plods on.
Carries on.

No longer the shy boy
I'm confident now.
But still not a biker, I never learned how.

I don't care.
I don't care.

She married the lad
With the bike in the end.
But I still always wonder if I could contend.

I don't know.
I don't know.

But if I knew then
What I know right now.
I'd have been a teenage dad and a granddad by now.

Oh I would.
Oh I would.

I'd have been through the school
Like a dose of the clap.
Didn't care about condoms or cervical caps.

I daren't think.
I daren't think.

At the time it wasn't easy
But I think it turned out right.
I've never had an STD and my bits still look alright.

I think I'll do.
I think I'll do.

Darren Whitehead

Old Grey Whistle

You could hear him before you saw him
Wheezing as he took every step and puffed smoke
He'll always be remembered
The old grey whistling man
With whiskers spouting from ears
The size of frying pan

You could hear him before you saw him
Clattering clog irons on cobbles, auld Sam
He wasn't the type to complain
A very reticent man

But don't have doubts about him
Nor the ashes in that jar
That's what you can hear wheezing
Although it sounds from afar

He really wanted to be buried
In his owld grey whistle and flute
But you wanted him brunt
You'd pawned that owld grey suit

He'll come back to haunt you, Mary
He towld me before he went
When you hear the clog irons
And wheezing
Its auld Sam,
Coming back, as he meant

Jeff Whitehead

Slurping

I'm not dead, I'm not alive
Stuck in the dark from nine till five
I don't hurt, I don't feel
I don't cry, or squeal.
I'm yours whenever you need
My white smooth body,
Your desires I feed.

My swan like neck, you take a grip
On my lip you place your lip.
All the slurping I endure
Sticky mess on my exterior.
A quick bath, I do enjoy
Before you close the prison door.

Left on the shelf with willow patterned lasses,
Flowery patterned dress, gold rimmed glasses.
Liquid flows in and out of me,
I'm your mug, your mug for tea.

Jeff Whitehead

Did I Just Say That?

Did I just say that?
Turn back the clock
My mouth just runs away.

I never meant to make you cry
Oh, darling, not today.

If my arms could stretch a hundred miles
I'd squeeze you, hold you close.
But your voice sounds cold on the telephone
And you don't have me engrossed.

Did I just say that?
No, it's too late.
My mouth just runs away.

I never meant to p*** you off,
Don't hang up, baby, stay.

If my smile could stretch a hundred miles
You'd know my heart is true.
But your telephone voice don't turn me on
So what am I supposed to do?

Did I just say that?
Oh no! My mouth!
Verbal diaorreah's here to stay.

I didn't want to make you angry
Honey, what can I say?

I'd gladly run a hundred miles
Just to feel your warm embrace
Cause I cannot picture on the telephone
The wrinkles on your face.

Did I just say that?
Oh I'm sorry I am
My mouth's in disarray.

I never meant to make you feel bad
So darling don't dismay.

I'd walk on coals a hundred miles
Until I was close to death.
To sleep beside you through the night
And smell your morning breath.

Did I just say that?
I just don't believe
That I cannot convey.

I don't want for us to fall out baby
And I hope that we're ok.

I'd swim a hundred miles to feel
Your lips against my lips.
And feel my hungry hands upon
Your buxom ample hips.

Did I just say that?
I think that it's time
To put down the telephone.

Before I completely
Mess up my life
And end up on my own!

Darren Whitehead

Thank Heathens for Festivity

Let me celebrate
Let me celebrate
Celebrate what I don't know.
Celebrate what I don't believe
Celebrate although

I know nothing of religion
Religion knows not me.
But Yuletide drinking,
Falling down
What festivity.

I drink I fall,
I clamber.
I clamber and I trip.
The shepherd's flock
Of drunken sheep
Sing from sleeping lip.

Let me celebrate
Let me celebrate
Celebrate what I don't know.
Celebrate what I don't believe
Celebrate although

I know not a lot of Easter,
Bank holidays are fine
Chocolate eggs,
A long weekend
A drink or two of wine.

Sick from cocoa sugar,
Sick from lack of sleep.
A bloody good Friday, we all had,
Me and the other sheep.

Let me celebrate a furry mouth,
Celebrate a banging head.
Celebrate a birth and celebrate
When someone's dead.

Celebrate a wedding,
A stag do, one last night.
Freedom of divorce,
Let's celebrate, it's only right!

A leaving party,
Celebrate.
Celebrate when someone's gone.
Celebrate new starters,
Celebrate when they move on.

I'll raise a glass to anything,
Drink to congratulation.
I'll drink to this,
I'll drink to that,
I'll drink to celebration.

                                        Darren Whitehead

My Daughter is an Angel:
(Try to read this with a West Country accent).

I'm really not a moaner,
And I'm not one for s**te.
But don't you dare come near my daughter,
Not any f*****g night!

My daughter is my angel,
She's mine and mine alone.
She doesn't want a city boy,
With your suit and mobile 'phone.

Now I don't care for city folk.
You don't know country ways.
You smoke your marijuana,
And set my crops ablaze.

My daughter is my angel,
She's pure as driven snow.
To find a better farmhand,
You'd have a way to go.

So take your pack of condoms,
And stick 'em up you're ass.
Go on, f**k off, you city boy,
Go smoke your bloody grass.

Cause if you come near my daughter,
You'll make me feel quite bitter.
I'll take my farmyard shotgun,
And shoot you up your s***ter!

My daughter is an angel,
She doesn't need no other.
She's happy in the hay barn,
With her cousin and her brother.

Darren Whitehead

Flat Caps & Braces

Flat caps and braces, white vests as well,
Ready and waiting, for the old fire bell.

All six moustaches, way overgrown,
These were stern men, the villagers' own.

Flat caps and braces, white vests as well,
Ready and waiting, for the old fire bell.

Ladders and wagons, on the alert,
Hosepipes in hand, ready to spurt.

Flat caps and braces, white vests as well,
Running in zigzags to the old fire bell.

A tipple they'd had, praying for rain.
Connected the hosepipe to the bloody gas main.

Flat caps and braces, black vests as well.
Staggering and swaggering to the old fire-bell.

Blew up the village, whole place in ashes,
Only thing left six bushy moustaches, plus

Flat caps and braces, singed vests as well,
Trouble and rubble, and a silent fire bell.

Jeff Whitehead

Miss Me Madly

I know its stress
The dripping tap
The cracked pane
Leaking roof
Gutters gone
Needs new doors
Rotting floors

Got no money
Need some clothes
Kid's school uniform
Need some specs
Need some teeth

Springs pushing their way through
Feel like a fucking jack in a box sat in this chair
Got no fags
Darn me socks
Shoes need mending
Am on the rocks

Dogs got worms
Cats got mange
Budgies going blind
If I had a shilling for't gas
I'd commit fucking suicide

Ain't even got a washer for't tap
Can't afford a pane of glass
Can't go on roof got bad knees
Tried mend gutter, rotted in my hand
Fell int' flipping fish pond

Anyway like I said
I know you'll miss me madly
But am leaving yer.

Jeff Whitehead

Rebel Without a Clue

Early finish today. Machines wind down at 2pm
Jack the lad shouts 'Hello my little gem'.
The girl giggles, wriggles, throws him a glance

'How you fixed for Christmas Eve dance?'
He flashes a wink,
'You're married,' she says,
'What do you think?'

Off to the pub to sink one or two,
What to buy wife he hasn't a clue.
He trudges to the bar
With frying pan and kettle too.

'These'll mek her smile', he laughs to a mate.
'Met mek her scrike. God help thi fate'

His wife watches clock, drinks glass of wine.
'Time he was home, the drunken swine'.

Blonde hair in curls, she wears a red dress,
Children asleep in bed, God bless.
It's getting late, there's going to be scorn,
Jack strolls through door 1am Christmas morn.

He lands on the lawn, face black and blue,
Lay just beside him, frying pan, kettle too.

Jeff Whitehead

www.ingramcontent.com/pod-product-compliance
Ingram Content Group UK Ltd.
Pitfield, Milton Keynes, MK11 3LW, UK
UKHW041434180426
11947UKWH00007B/437